ESSENTIAL

EUROPEAN SHOPPERS' CONVERSION GUIDE

ANTHEA NICHOLS

GW00363088

Published by
Boatswain Press Ltd
Dudley House, 12 North Street
Emsworth, Hampshire PO10 7DQ
telephone 0243-377977

© Anthea Nichols 1993
The right of Anthea Nichols to be identified as the author of this
work has been asserted in accordance with the Copyright, Designs
and Patents Act 1988

All rights reserved. No part of this publication may be repro-
duced, stored in a retrieval system, or transmitted in any form or
by any means, electronic, mechanical, photocopying, recording or
otherwise, without the prior permission of the copyright owner

Cover design, Slatter Anderson
Illustrations by Teri Gower
Printed in Great Britain

British Library Cataloguing-in-Publication Data
A catalogue record for this book is available from the British
Library
ISBN 1 873432 43 7

CONTENTS

AREA CONVERSION TABLES

CLOTHES SIZE CONVERSION TABLES

COMPARATIVE PRICE TABLES

DISTANCE CONVERSION TABLES

ENERGY CONVERSION TABLES

PRESSURE CONVERSION TABLES

SPEED CONVERSION TABLES

TEMPERATURE CONVERSION TABLES

VOLUME CONVERSION TABLES

WEIGHT CONVERSION TABLES

AREA
CONVERSION
TABLES

SQUARE INCHES TO SQUARE MILLIMETRES *multiply by 645.20*		SQUARE MILLIMETRES TO SQUARE INCHES *multiply by 0.0016*	
sq ins	sq mms	sq mms	sq ins
0.25	161.30	0.25	0.00
0.5	322.60	0.5	0.00
0.75	483.90	0.75	0.00
1	645.20	1	0.00
2	1290.40	2	0.00
3	1935.60	3	0.00
4	2580.80	4	0.01
5	3226.00	5	0.01
6	3871.20	6	0.01
7	4516.40	7	0.01
8	5161.60	8	0.01
9	5806.80	9	0.01
10	6452.00	10	0.02
11	7097.20	11	0.02
12	7742.40	12	0.02

sq ins	sq mms	sq mms	sq ins
13	8387.60	13	0.02
14	9032.80	14	0.02
15	9678.00	15	0.02
16	10323.20	16	0.02
17	10968.40	17	0.03
18	11613.60	18	0.03
19	12258.80	19	0.03
20	12904.00	20	0.03
25	16130.00	25	0.04
30	19356.00	30	0.05
35	22582.00	35	0.05
40	25808.00	40	0.06
45	29034.00	45	0.07
50	32260.00	50	0.08
60	38712.00	60	0.09
70	45164.00	70	0.11
80	51616.00	80	0.12
90	58068.00	90	0.14
100	64520.00	100	0.16

SQUARE INCHES TO SQUARE CENTIMETRES *multiply by 6.4520*		SQUARE CENTIMETRES TO SQUARE INCHES *multiply by 0.1550*	
sq ins	sq cms	sq cms	sq ins
0.25	1.61	0.25	0.04
0.5	3.23	0.5	0.08
0.75	4.84	0.75	0.12
1	6.45	1	0.16
2	12.90	2	0.31
3	19.36	3	0.47
4	25.81	4	0.62
5	32.26	5	0.78
6	38.71	6	0.93
7	45.16	7	1.09
8	51.62	8	1.24
9	58.07	9	1.40
10	64.52	10	1.55
11	70.97	11	1.71
12	77.42	12	1.86

sq ins	sq cms	sq cms	sq ins
13	83.88	13	2.02
14	90.33	14	2.17
15	96.78	15	2.33
16	103.23	16	2.48
17	109.68	17	2.64
18	116.14	18	2.79
19	122.59	19	2.95
20	129.04	20	3.10
25	161.30	25	3.88
30	193.56	30	4.65
35	225.82	35	5.43
40	258.08	40	6.20
45	290.34	45	6.98
50	322.60	50	7.75
60	387.12	60	9.30
70	451.64	70	10.85
80	516.16	80	12.40
90	580.68	90	13.95
100	645.20	100	15.50

SQUARE FEET TO SQUARE METRES		SQUARE METRES TO SQUARE FEET	
multiply by 0.0929		*multiply by 10.7640*	
sq ft	sq ms	sq ms	sq ft
0.25	0.02	0.25	2.69
0.5	0.05	0.5	5.38
0.75	0.07	0.75	8.07
1	0.09	1	10.76
2	0.19	2	21.53
3	0.28	3	32.29
4	0.37	4	43.06
5	0.46	5	53.82
6	0.56	6	64.58
7	0.65	7	75.35
8	0.74	8	86.11
9	0.84	9	96.88
10	0.93	10	107.64
11	1.02	11	118.40
12	1.11	12	129.17

sq ft	sq ms	sq ms	sq ft
13	1.21	13	139.93
14	1.30	14	150.70
15	1.39	15	161.46
16	1.49	16	172.22
17	1.58	17	182.99
18	1.67	18	193.75
19	1.77	19	204.52
20	1.86	20	215.28
25	2.32	25	269.10
30	2.79	30	322.92
35	3.25	35	376.74
40	3.72	40	430.56
45	4.18	45	484.38
50	4.65	50	538.20
60	5.57	60	645.84
70	6.50	70	753.48
80	7.43	80	861.12
90	8.36	90	968.76
100	9.29	100	1076.40

SQUARE YARDS TO SQUARE METRES		SQUARE METRES TO SQUARE YARDS	
multiply by 0.8361		*multiply by 1.1960*	
sq yds	sq ms	sq ms	sq yds
0.25	0.21	0.25	0.30
0.5	0.42	0.5	0.60
0.75	0.63	0.75	0.90
1	0.84	1	1.20
2	1.67	2	2.39
3	2.51	3	3.59
4	3.34	4	4.78
5	4.18	5	5.98
6	5.02	6	7.18
7	5.85	7	8.37
8	6.69	8	9.57
9	7.52	9	10.76
10	8.36	10	11.96
11	9.20	11	13.16
12	10.03	12	14.35

sq yds	sq ms	sq ms	sq yds
13	10.87	13	15.55
14	11.71	14	16.74
15	12.54	15	17.94
16	13.38	16	19.14
17	14.21	17	20.33
18	15.05	18	21.53
19	15.89	19	22.72
20	16.72	20	23.92
25	20.90	25	29.90
30	25.08	30	35.88
35	29.26	35	41.86
40	33.44	40	47.84
45	37.62	45	53.82
50	41.81	50	59.80
60	50.17	60	71.76
70	58.53	70	83.72
80	66.89	80	95.68
90	75.25	90	107.64
100	83.61	100	119.60

SQUARE MILES TO SQUARE KILOMETRES		SQUARE KILOMETRES TO SQUARE MILES	
multiply by 2.5900		*multiply by 0.3861*	
sq miles	sq kms	sq kms	sq miles
0.25	0.65	0.25	0.30
0.5	1.30	0.5	0.60
0.75	1.94	0.75	0.90
1	2.59	1	1.20
2	5.18	2	2.39
3	7.77	3	3.59
4	10.36	4	4.78
5	12.95	5	5.98
6	15.54	6	7.18
7	18.13	7	8.37
8	20.72	8	9.57
9	23.31	9	10.76
10	25.90	10	11.96
11	28.49	11	13.16
12	31.08	12	14.35

sq miles	sq kms	sq kms	sq miles
13	33.67	13	15.55
14	36.26	14	16.74
15	38.85	15	17.94
16	41.44	16	19.14
17	44.03	17	20.33
18	46.62	18	21.53
19	49.21	19	22.72
20	51.80	20	23.92
25	64.75	25	29.90
30	77.70	30	35.88
35	90.65	35	41.86
40	103.60	40	47.84
45	116.55	45	53.82
50	129.50	50	59.80
60	155.40	60	71.76
70	181.30	70	83.72
80	207.20	80	95.68
90	233.10	90	107.64
100	259.00	100	119.60

ACRES TO HECTARES

HECTARES TO ACRES

multiply by 0.4047

multiply by 2.4710

acres	hectares	hectares	acres
0.25	0.10	0.25	0.62
0.5	0.20	0.5	1.24
0.75	0.30	0.75	1.85
1	0.40	1	2.47
2	0.81	2	4.94
3	1.21	3	7.41
4	1.62	4	9.88
5	2.02	5	12.36
6	2.43	6	14.83
7	2.83	7	17.30
8	3.24	8	19.77
9	3.64	9	22.24
10	4.05	10	24.71
11	4.45	11	27.18
12	4.86	12	29.65

acres	hectares	hectares	acres
13	5.26	13	32.12
14	5.67	14	34.59
15	6.07	15	37.07
16	6.48	16	39.54
17	6.88	17	42.01
18	7.28	18	44.48
19	7.69	19	46.95
20	8.09	20	49.42
25	10.12	25	61.78
30	12.14	30	74.13
35	14.16	35	86.49
40	16.19	40	98.84
45	18.21	45	111.20
50	20.24	50	123.55
60	24.28	60	148.26
70	28.33	70	172.97
80	32.38	80	197.68
90	36.42	90	222.39
100	40.47	100	247.10

CLOTHES SIZE
CONVERSION
TABLES

CHILDRENS CLOTHES

The 'centilong' system is used for determining the sizes of children's clothes.
The following sizes correspond to the child's height in centimetres.

Baby	62	68	74	80	86
Infant	92	98	104	110	
School-age child	116	122	128	134	140	146
Teenager	152	158	164	167	

HAT SIZES

UK	France	Metric
$5^{7}/_{8}$	½	48
6	1	49
$6^{1}/_{8}$	1½	50
6¼	2	51
$6^{3}/_{8}$	2½	52
6½	3	53
$6^{5}/_{8}$	3½	54
6¾	4	55
$6^{7}/_{8}$	4½	56
7	5	57
$7^{1}/_{8}$	5½	58
7¼	6	59
$7^{3}/_{8}$	6½	60
7½	7	61
$7^{5}/_{8}$	7½	62
7¾	8	63
$7^{7}/_{8}$	8½	64

MENS CLOTHES – AVERAGE LENGTH

	UK	Germany	Spain	France	Belgium	Italy	Sweden
size	34	44	44/6	44-38	44	44	C44
size	36	44	46/6	46-40	46	46	C46
size	38	48	48/6	48-42	48	48	C48
size	40	50	50/6	50-44	50	50	C50
size	42	52	52	52-46	52	52	C52
size	44	54	54/6	54-48	54	54	C54
size	46	56	56/6	56-50	56	56	C56
size	48	58		58-52	58	58	C58
size	50	60		60-54		60	60

21

WOMENS CLOTHES

	UK	Germany	Spain	France	Portugal	Italy	Sweden
size	8	34	36	34	36	38	34
bust (cm)	80	80	78	81	78	82	81
hips (cm)	85	85	84	89	84	84	89
size	10	36	38	36	38	40	36
bust (cm)	82	84	82	84	82	85	84
hips (cm)	87	90	88	92	88	88	92
size	12	38	40	38	40	42	38
bust (cm)	87	88	86	87	86	88	87
hips (cm)	92	94	92	95	92	92	95

	UK	Germany	Spain	France	Portugal	Italy	Sweden
size	14	40	42	40	42	44	40
bust (cm)	92	92	90	90	90	91	90
hips (cm)	97	98	96	98	96	96	98
size	16	42	44	42	44	46	42
bust (cm)	97	96	94	93	94	94	94
hips (cm)	102	102	100	101	100	100	102
size	18	44	46	44	46	48	44
bust (cm)	102	100	96	96	97	97	98
hips (cm)	109	106	104	104	104	104	106
size	20	46	46	46	48	50	46
bust (cm)	109	104	104	99	104	100	103
hips (cm)	114	110	110	107	110	108	111

SHOE SIZES

WOMENS

UK	Europe
2	34
2½	34½
3	35
3½	35½
4	36½
4½	37
5	37½
5½	38
6	39
6½	39½
7	40½
7½	41
8	41½

MENS

UK	Europe
4½	37½
5	38
5½	38½
6	39½
6½	40
7	40½
7½	41
8	42
8½	42½
9	43
9½	43½
10	44
10½	44½

CHILDRENS

UK	Europe	UK	Europe
0	15	7	24
1	17	8	25
2	18	8½	26
3	19	9	27
4	20	10	28
4½	21	11	29
5	22	12	30
6	23	12½	31

COMPARATIVE
PRICE
TABLES

PRICE PER PINT TO PRICE PER LITRE		PRICE PER POUND TO PRICE PER KILOGRAMME	
per pt	per ltr	per lb	per kg
3 p	5 p	7 p	15 p
5 p	9 p	9 p	20 p
7 p	12 p	10 p	22 p
9 p	16 p	12 p	26 p
10 p	18 p	14 p	31 p
12 p	21 p	16 p	35 p
14 p	25 p	18 p	40 p
16 p	28 p	20 p	44 p
18 p	32 p	21 p	46 p
20 p	35 p	23 p	51 p
21 p	37 p	25 p	55 p
23 p	40 p	27 p	60 p
25 p	44 p	29 p	64 p
27 p	48 p	30 p	66 p
29 p	51 p	35 p	77 p

per pt	per ltr	per lb	per kg
30 p	53 p	40p	88 p
35 p	62 p	45 p	99 p
40 p	70 p	50 p	1.10 p
45 p	79 p	55 p	1.21 p
50 p	88 p	60 p	1.32 p
55 p	97 p	65 p	1.43 p
60 p	1.06 p	70 p	1.54 p
65 p	1.14 p	75 p	1.65 p
70 p	1.23 p	80 p	1.76 p
75 p	1.32 p	85 p	1.87 p
80 p	1.41 p	90 p	1.98 p
85 p	1.50 p	95 p	2.09 p
90 p	1.58 p	1.00 p	2.21 p
95 p	1.67 p	1.10 p	2.43 p
1.00 p	1.76 p	1.20 p	2.65 p
1.10 p	1.94 p	1.40 p	3.09 p
1.20 p	2.11 p	1.60 p	3.53 p
1.30 p	2.29 p	1.80 p	3.97 p
1.40 p	2.46 p	2.00 p	4.41 p
1.50 p	2.64 p	2.50 p	5.51 p

DISTANCE
CONVERSION
TABLES

INCHES TO MILLIMETRES

MILLIMETRES TO INCHES

multiply by 25.4000

multiply by 0.0394

ins	mms	mms	ins
0.25	6.35	0.25	0.01
0.5	12.70	0.5	0.02
0.75	19.05	0.75	0.03
1	25.40	1	0.04
2	50.80	2	0.08
3	76.20	3	0.12
4	101.60	4	0.16
5	127.00	5	0.20
6	152.40	6	0.24
7	177.80	7	0.28
8	203.20	8	0.31
9	228.60	9	0.35
10	254.00	10	0.39
11	279.40	11	0.43
12	304.80	12	0.47

ins	mms	mms	ins
13	330.20	13	0.51
14	355.60	14	0.55
15	381.00	15	0.59
16	406.40	16	0.63
17	431.80	17	0.67
18	457.20	18	0.71
19	482.60	19	0.75
20	508.00	20	0.79
25	635.00	25	0.98
30	762.00	30	1.18
35	889.00	35	1.38
40	1016.00	40	1.57
45	1143.00	45	1.77
50	1270.00	50	1.97
60	1524.00	60	2.36
70	1778.00	70	2.76
80	2032.00	80	3.15
90	2286.00	90	3.54
100	2540.00	100	3.94

INCHES TO CENTIMETRES

CENTIMETRES TO INCHES

multiply by 2.5400

multiply by 0.3937

ins	cms	cms	ins
0.25	0.64	0.25	0.10
0.5	1.27	0.5	0.20
0.75	1.91	0.75	0.30
1	2.54	1	0.39
2	5.08	2	0.79
3	7.62	3	1.18
4	10.16	4	1.57
5	12.70	5	1.97
6	15.24	6	2.36
7	17.78	7	2.76
8	20.32	8	3.15
9	22.86	9	3.54
10	25.40	10	3.94
11	27.94	11	4.33
12	30.48	12	4.72

ins	cms	cms	ins
13	33.02	13	5.12
14	35.56	14	5.51
15	38.10	15	5.91
16	40.64	16	6.30
17	43.18	17	6.69
18	45.72	18	7.09
19	48.26	19	7.48
20	50.80	20	7.87
25	63.50	25	9.84
30	76.20	30	11.81
35	88.90	35	13.78
40	101.60	40	15.75
45	114.30	45	17.72
50	127.00	50	19.69
60	152.40	60	23.62
70	177.80	70	27.56
80	203.20	80	31.50
90	228.60	90	35.43
100	254.00	100	39.37

FEET TO METRES

METRES TO FEET

multiply by 0.3048

multiply by 3.2810

feet	metres	metres	feet
0.25	0.08	0.25	0.82
0.5	0.15	0.5	1.64
0.75	0.23	0.75	2.46
1	0.30	1	3.28
2	0.61	2	6.56
3	0.91	3	9.84
4	1.22	4	13.12
5	1.52	5	16.41
6	1.83	6	19.69
7	2.13	7	22.97
8	2.44	8	26.25
9	2.74	9	29.53
10	3.05	10	32.81
11	3.35	11	36.09
12	3.66	12	39.37

feet	metres	metres	feet
13	3.96	13	42.65
14	4.27	14	45.93
15	4.57	15	49.22
16	4.88	16	52.50
17	5.18	17	55.78
18	5.49	18	59.06
19	5.79	19	62.34
20	6.10	20	65.62
25	7.62	25	82.03
30	9.14	30	98.43
35	10.67	35	114.84
40	12.19	40	131.24
45	13.72	45	147.65
50	15.24	50	164.05
60	18.29	60	196.86
70	21.34	70	229.67
80	24.38	80	262.48
90	27.43	90	295.29
100	30.48	100	328.10

YARDS TO METRES

METRES TO YARDS

multiply by 0.9144

multiply by 1.0940

yards	metres	metres	yards
0.25	0.23	0.25	0.27
0.5	0.46	0.5	0.55
0.75	0.69	0.75	0.82
1	0.91	1	1.09
2	1.83	2	2.19
3	2.74	3	3.28
4	3.66	4	4.38
5	4.57	5	5.47
6	5.49	6	6.56
7	6.40	7	7.66
8	7.32	8	8.75
9	8.23	9	9.85
10	9.14	10	10.94
11	10.06	11	12.03
12	10.97	12	13.13

yards	metres	metres	yards
13	11.89	13	14.22
14	12.80	14	15.32
15	13.72	15	16.41
16	14.63	16	17.50
17	15.54	17	18.60
18	16.46	18	19.69
19	17.37	19	20.79
20	18.29	20	21.88
25	22.86	25	27.35
30	27.43	30	32.82
35	32.00	35	38.29
40	36.58	40	43.76
45	41.15	45	49.23
50	45.72	50	54.70
60	54.86	60	65.64
70	64.01	70	76.58
80	73.15	80	87.52
90	82.30	90	98.46
100	91.44	100	109.40

MILES TO KILOMETRES

KILOMETRES TO MILES

multiply by 1.6090

multiply by 0.6214

miles	kms	kms	miles
0.25	0.40	0.25	0.16
0.5	0.80	0.5	0.31
0.75	1.21	0.75	0.47
1	1.61	1	0.62
2	3.22	2	1.24
3	4.83	3	1.86
4	6.44	4	2.49
5	8.05	5	3.11
6	9.65	6	3.73
7	11.26	7	4.35
8	12.87	8	4.97
9	14.48	9	5.59
10	16.09	10	6.21
11	17.70	11	6.84
12	19.31	12	7.46

miles	kms	kms	miles
13	20.92	13	8.08
14	22.53	14	8.70
15	24.14	15	9.32
16	25.74	16	9.94
17	27.35	17	10.56
18	28.96	18	11.19
19	30.57	19	11.81
20	32.18	20	12.43
25	40.23	25	15.54
30	48.27	30	18.64
35	56.32	35	21.75
40	64.36	40	24.86
45	72.41	45	27.96
50	80.45	50	31.07
60	96.54	60	37.28
70	112.63	70	43.50
80	128.72	80	49.71
90	144.81	90	55.93
100	160.90	100	62.14

NAUTICAL MILES TO KILOMETRES

KILOMETRES TO NAUTICAL MILES

multiply by 1.8520

multiply by 0.5400

nt miles	kms	kms	nt miles
0.25	0.46	0.25	0.14
0.5	0.93	0.5	0.27
0.75	1.39	0.75	0.41
1	1.85	1	0.54
2	3.70	2	1.08
3	5.56	3	1.62
4	7.41	4	2.16
5	9.26	5	2.70
6	11.11	6	3.24
7	12.96	7	3.78
8	14.82	8	4.32
9	16.67	9	4.86
10	18.52	10	5.40
11	20.37	11	5.94
12	22.22	12	6.48

nt miles	kms	kms	nt miles
13	24.08	13	7.02
14	25.93	14	7.56
15	27.78	15	8.10
16	29.63	16	8.64
17	31.48	17	9.18
18	33.34	18	9.72
19	35.19	19	10.26
20	37.04	20	10.80
25	46.30	25	13.50
30	55.56	30	16.20
35	64.82	35	18.90
40	74.08	40	21.60
45	83.34	45	24.30
50	92.60	50	27.00
60	111.12	60	32.40
70	129.64	70	37.80
80	148.16	80	43.20
90	166.68	90	48.60
100	185.20	100	54.00

ENERGY
CONVERSION
TABLES

CALORIES TO JOULES

JOULES TO CALORIES

multiply by 4.1868

multiply by 0.2385

calories	joules	joules	calories
0.25	1.05	0.25	0.06
0.5	2.09	0.5	0.12
0.75	3.14	0.75	0.18
1	4.19	1	0.24
2	8.37	2	0.48
3	12.56	3	0.72
4	16.75	4	0.95
5	20.93	5	1.19
6	25.12	6	1.43
7	29.31	7	1.67
8	33.49	8	1.91
9	37.68	9	2.15
10	41.87	10	2.39
11	46.05	11	2.62
12	50.24	12	2.86

calories	joules	joules	calories
13	54.43	13	3.10
14	58.62	14	3.34
15	62.80	15	3.58
16	66.99	16	3.82
17	71.18	17	4.05
18	75.36	18	4.29
19	79.55	19	4.53
20	83.74	20	4.77
25	104.67	25	5.96
30	125.60	30	7.16
35	146.54	35	8.35
40	167.47	40	9.54
45	188.41	45	10.73
50	209.34	50	11.93
60	251.21	60	14.31
70	293.08	70	16.70
80	334.94	80	19.08
90	376.81	90	21.47
100	418.68	100	23.85

HP TO METRIC HORSEPOWER

METRIC HORSEPOWER TO HP

multiply by 1.014   *multiply by 0.9862*

hp	metric hp	metric hp	hp
0.25	0.25	0.25	0.25
0.5	0.51	0.5	0.49
0.75	0.76	0.75	0.74
1	1.01	1	0.99
2	2.03	2	1.97
3	3.04	3	2.96
4	4.06	4	3.94
5	5.07	5	4.93
6	6.08	6	5.92
7	7.10	7	6.90
8	8.11	8	7.89
9	9.13	9	8.88
10	10.14	10	9.86
11	11.15	11	10.85
12	12.17	12	11.83

hp	metric hp	metric hp	hp
13	13.18	13	12.82
14	14.20	14	13.81
15	15.21	15	14.79
16	16.22	16	15.78
17	17.24	17	16.77
18	18.25	18	17.75
19	19.27	19	18.74
20	20.28	20	19.72
25	25.35	25	24.66
30	30.42	30	29.59
35	35.49	35	34.52
40	40.56	40	39.45
45	45.63	45	44.38
50	50.70	50	49.31
60	60.84	60	59.17
70	70.98	70	69.03
80	81.12	80	78.90
90	91.26	90	88.76
100	101.40	100	98.62

HORSEPOWER TO KILOWATTS

multiply by 0.7457

KILOWATTS TO HORSEPOWER

multiply by 1.341

hp	kwatts	kwatts	hp
0.25	0.19	0.25	0.34
0.5	0.37	0.5	0.67
0.75	0.56	0.75	1.01
1	0.75	1	1.34
2	1.49	2	2.68
3	2.24	3	4.02
4	2.98	4	5.36
5	3.73	5	6.71
6	4.47	6	8.05
7	5.22	7	9.39
8	5.97	8	10.73
9	6.71	9	12.07
10	7.46	10	13.41
11	8.20	11	14.75
12	8.95	12	16.09

hp	kwatts	kwatts	hp
13	9.69	13	17.43
14	10.44	14	18.77
15	11.19	15	20.12
16	11.93	16	21.46
17	12.68	17	22.80
18	13.42	18	24.14
19	14.17	19	25.48
20	14.91	20	26.82
25	18.64	25	33.53
30	22.37	30	40.23
35	26.10	35	46.94
40	29.83	40	53.64
45	33.56	45	60.35
50	37.29	50	67.05
60	44.74	60	80.46
70	52.20	70	93.87
80	59.66	80	107.28
90	67.11	90	120.69
100	74.57	100	134.10

PRESSURE
CONVERSION
TABLES

POUNDS PER SQ INCH TO KILOS PER SQ CENTIMETRE *multiply by 0.0703*		KILOS PER SQ CENTIMETRE TO POUNDS PER SQ INCH *multiply by 14.2200*	
lb/sq in	kg/sq cm	kg/sq cm	lb/sq in
0.25	0.02	0.25	3.56
0.5	0.04	0.5	7.11
0.75	0.05	0.75	10.67
1	0.07	1	14.22
2	0.14	2	28.44
3	0.21	3	42.66
4	0.28	4	56.88
5	0.35	5	71.10
6	0.42	6	85.32
7	0.49	7	99.54
8	0.56	8	113.76
9	0.63	9	127.98
10	0.70	10	142.20
11	0.77	11	156.42
12	0.84	12	170.64

lb/sq in	kg/sq cm	kg/sq cm	lb/sq in
13	0.91	13	184.86
14	0.98	14	199.08
15	1.05	15	213.30
16	1.12	16	227.52
17	1.20	17	241.74
18	1.27	18	255.96
19	1.34	19	270.18
20	1.41	20	284.40
25	1.76	25	355.50
30	2.11	30	426.60
35	2.46	35	497.70
40	2.81	40	568.80
45	3.16	45	639.90
50	3.52	50	711.00
60	4.22	60	853.20
70	4.92	70	995.40
80	5.62	80	1137.60
90	6.33	90	1279.80
100	7.03	100	1422.00

SPEED
CONVERSION
TABLES

FEET PER SECOND TO METRES PER SECOND *multiply by 0.3048*		METRES PER SECOND TO FEETPER SECOND *multiply by 3.2810*	
ft/sec	met/sec	met/sec	ft/sec
0.25	0.08	0.25	0.82
0.5	0.15	0.5	1.64
0.75	0.23	0.75	2.46
1	0.30	1	3.28
2	0.61	2	6.56
3	0.91	3	9.84
4	1.22	4	13.12
5	1.52	5	16.41
6	1.83	6	19.69
7	2.13	7	22.97
8	2.44	8	26.25
9	2.74	9	29.53
10	3.05	10	32.81
11	3.35	11	36.09
12	3.66	12	39.37

ft/sec	met/sec	met/sec	ft/sec
13	3.96	13	42.65
14	4.27	14	45.93
15	4.57	15	49.22
16	4.88	16	52.50
17	5.18	17	55.78
18	5.49	18	59.06
19	5.79	19	62.34
20	6.10	20	65.62
25	7.62	25	82.03
30	9.14	30	98.43
35	10.67	35	114.84
40	12.19	40	131.24
45	13.72	45	147.65
50	15.24	50	164.05
60	18.29	60	196.86
70	21.34	70	229.67
80	24.38	80	262.48
90	27.43	90	295.29
100	30.48	100	328.10

FEET PER SECOND TO MILES PER HOUR		MILES PER HOUR TO FEET PER SECOND	
multiply by 0.6820		*multiply by 1.467*	
ft/sec	mph	mph	ft/sec
0.25	0.17	0.25	0.37
0.5	0.34	0.5	0.73
0.75	0.51	0.75	1.10
1	0.68	1	1.47
2	1.36	2	2.93
3	2.05	3	4.40
4	2.73	4	5.87
5	3.41	5	7.34
6	4.09	6	8.80
7	4.77	7	10.27
8	5.46	8	11.74
9	6.14	9	13.20
10	6.82	10	14.67
11	7.50	11	16.14
12	8.18	12	17.60

ft/sec	mph	mph	ft/sec
13	8.87	13	19.07
14	9.55	14	20.54
15	10.23	15	22.01
16	10.91	16	23.47
17	11.59	17	24.94
18	12.28	18	26.41
19	12.96	19	27.87
20	13.64	20	29.34
25	17.05	25	36.68
30	20.46	30	44.01
35	23.87	35	51.35
40	27.28	40	58.68
45	30.69	45	66.02
50	34.10	50	73.35
60	40.92	60	88.02
70	47.74	70	102.69
80	54.56	80	117.36
90	61.38	90	132.03
100	68.20	100	146.70

MILES PER HOUR TO KILOMETRES PER HOUR		KILOMETRES PER HOUR TO MILES PER HOUR	
multiply by 1.6090		*multiply by 0.6214*	
mph	kph	kph	mph
0.25	0.40	0.25	0.16
0.5	0.80	0.5	0.31
0.75	1.21	0.75	0.47
1	1.61	1	0.62
2	3.22	2	1.24
3	4.83	3	1.86
4	6.44	4	2.49
5	8.05	5	3.11
6	9.65	6	3.73
7	11.26	7	4.35
8	12.87	8	4.97
9	14.48	9	5.59
10	16.09	10	6.21
11	17.70	11	6.84
12	19.31	12	7.46

mph	kph	kph	mph
13	20.92	13	8.08
14	22.53	14	8.70
15	24.14	15	9.32
16	25.74	16	9.94
17	27.35	17	10.56
18	28.96	18	11.19
19	30.57	19	11.81
20	32.18	20	12.43
25	40.23	25	15.54
30	48.27	30	18.64
35	56.32	35	21.75
40	64.36	40	24.86
45	72.41	45	27.96
50	80.45	50	31.07
60	96.54	60	37.28
70	112.63	70	43.50
80	128.72	80	49.71
90	144.81	90	55.93
100	160.90	100	62.14

WIND SPEEDS

Force	Wind speed (knots)	Description
0	0-1	Calm
1	1-3	Light air
2	4-6	Light breeze
3	7-10	Gentle breeze
4	11-16	Moderate breeze
5	17-21	Fresh breeze
6	22-27	Strong breeze
7	28-33	Near gale
8	34-40	Gale
9	41-47	Severe gale
10	48-55	Storm
11	56-63	Violent storm
12	64 plus	Hurricane

TEMPERATURE
CONVERSION
TABLES

FAHRENHEIT TO CENTIGRADE

CENTIGRADE TO FAHRENHEIT

formula (F°-32)÷1.8

formula (C°x1.8)+32

F°	C°	C°	F°
-40	-40	-40	-40
-35	-37	-35	-31
-30	-34	-30	-22
-25	-32	-25	-13
-20	-29	-20	-4
-15	-26	-19	-2
-10	-23	-18	-0
-5	-21	-17	1
0	-18	-16	3
5	-15	-15	5
10	-12	-14	7
15	-9	-13	9
20	-7	-12	10
25	-4	-11	12
30	-1	-10	14

F°	C°	C°	F°
35	2	-9	16
40	4	-8	18
45	7	-7	19
50	10	-6	21
55	13	-5	23
60	16	-4	25
61	16	-3	27
62	17	-2	28
63	17	-1	30
64	18	0	32
65	18	1	34
66	19	2	36
67	19	3	37
68	20	4	39
69	21	5	41
70	21	6	43
71	22	7	45
72	22	8	46
73	23	9	48
74	23	10	50

F°	C°	C°	F°
75	24	11	52
76	24	12	54
77	25	13	55
78	26	14	57
79	26	15	59
80	27	16	61
81	27	17	63
82	28	18	64
83	28	19	66
84	29	20	68
85	29	21	70
86	30	22	72
87	31	23	73
88	31	24	75
89	32	25	77
90	32	26	79
91	33	27	81
92	33	28	82
93	34	29	84
94	34	30	86

F°	C°	C°	F°
95	35	31	88
96	36	32	90
97	36	33	91
98	37	34	93
99	37	35	95
100	38	36	97
101	38	37	99
102	39	38	100
103	39	39	102
104	40	40	104
105	41	41	106
106	41	42	108
107	42	43	109
108	42	44	111
109	43	45	113
110	43	46	115

OVEN TEMPERATURES

°F	°C	Gas Mark	Oven
200	93		**very cool**
225	107	¼	
250	121	½	
275	135	1	**cool**
300	149	2	
325	163	3	**moderate**
350	177	4	
375	191	5	**moderately hot**
400	204	6	
425	218	7	**hot**
450	232	8	
475	246	9	**very hot**
500	260		

VOLUME
CONVERSION
TABLES

CUBIC INCHES TO CUBIC CENTIMETRES *multiply by 16.3900*		CUBIC CENTIMETRES TO CUBIC INCHES *multiply by 0.0610*	
cu ins	cu cms	cu cms	cu ins
0.25	4.10	0.25	0.02
0.5	8.20	0.5	0.03
0.75	12.29	0.75	0.05
1	16.39	1	0.06
2	32.78	2	0.12
3	49.17	3	0.18
4	65.56	4	0.24
5	81.95	5	0.31
6	98.34	6	0.37
7	114.73	7	0.43
8	131.12	8	0.49
9	147.51	9	0.55
10	163.90	10	0.61
11	180.29	11	0.67
12	196.68	12	0.73

cu ins	cu cms	cu cms	cu ins
13	213.07	13	0.79
14	229.46	14	0.85
15	245.85	15	0.92
16	262.24	16	0.98
17	278.63	17	1.04
18	295.02	18	1.10
19	311.41	19	1.16
20	327.80	20	1.22
25	409.75	25	1.53
30	491.70	30	1.83
35	573.65	35	2.14
40	655.60	40	2.44
45	737.55	45	2.75
50	819.50	50	3.05
60	983.40	60	3.66
70	1147.30	70	4.27
80	1311.20	80	4.88
90	1475.10	90	5.49
100	1639.00	100	6.10

CUBIC FEET TO CUBIC METRES		CUBIC METRES TO CUBIC FEET	
multiply by 0.0283		*multiply by 35.3100*	
cu ft	cu ms	cu ms	cu ft
0.25	0.01	0.25	8.83
0.5	0.01	0.5	17.66
0.75	0.02	0.75	26.48
1	0.03	1	35.31
2	0.06	2	70.62
3	0.08	3	105.93
4	0.11	4	141.24
5	0.14	5	176.55
6	0.17	6	211.86
7	0.20	7	247.17
8	0.23	8	282.48
9	0.25	9	317.79
10	0.28	10	353.10
11	0.31	11	388.41
12	0.34	12	423.72

cu ft	cu ms	cu ms	cu ft
13	0.37	13	459.03
14	0.40	14	494.34
15	0.42	15	529.65
16	0.45	16	564.96
17	0.48	17	600.27
18	0.51	18	635.58
19	0.54	19	670.89
20	0.57	20	706.20
25	0.71	25	882.75
30	0.85	30	1059.30
35	0.99	35	1235.85
40	1.13	40	1412.40
45	1.27	45	1588.95
50	1.42	50	1765.50
60	1.70	60	2118.60
70	1.98	70	2471.70
80	2.26	80	2824.80
90	2.55	90	3177.90
100	2.83	100	3531.00

CUBIC YARDS TO CUBIC METRES		CUBIC METRES TO CUBIC YARDS	
multiply by 0.7646		*multiply by 1.3080*	
cu yds	cu ms	cu ms	cu yds
0.25	0.19	0.25	0.33
0.5	0.38	0.5	0.65
0.75	0.57	0.75	0.98
1	0.76	1	1.31
2	1.53	2	2.62
3	2.29	3	3.92
4	3.06	4	5.23
5	3.82	5	6.54
6	4.59	6	7.85
7	5.35	7	9.16
8	6.12	8	10.46
9	6.88	9	11.77
10	7.65	10	13.08
11	8.41	11	14.39
12	9.18	12	15.70

cu yds	cu ms	cu ms	cu yds
13	9.94	13	17.00
14	10.70	14	18.31
15	11.47	15	19.62
16	12.23	16	20.93
17	13.00	17	22.24
18	13.76	18	23.54
19	14.53	19	24.85
20	15.29	20	26.16
25	19.12	25	32.70
30	22.94	30	39.24
35	26.76	35	45.78
40	30.58	40	52.32
45	34.41	45	58.86
50	38.23	50	65.40
60	45.88	60	78.48
70	53.52	70	91.56
80	61.17	80	104.64
90	68.81	90	117.72
100	76.46	100	130.80

PINTS TO CENTILITRES

CENTILITRES TO PINTS

multiply by 56.80

multiply by 0.0176

pints	cls	cls	pints
0.25	14.20	0.25	0.00
0.5	28.40	0.5	0.01
0.75	42.60	0.75	0.01
1	56.80	1	0.02
2	113.60	2	0.04
3	170.40	3	0.05
4	227.20	4	0.07
5	284.00	5	0.09
6	340.80	6	0.11
7	397.60	7	0.12
8	454.40	8	0.14
9	511.20	9	0.16
10	568.00	10	0.18
11	624.80	11	0.19
12	681.60	12	0.21

pints	cl	cl	pints
13	738.40	13	0.23
14	795.20	14	0.25
15	852.00	15	0.26
16	908.80	16	0.28
17	965.60	17	0.30
18	1022.40	18	0.32
19	1079.20	19	0.33
20	1136.00	20	0.35
25	1420.00	25	0.44
30	1704.00	30	0.53
35	1988.00	35	0.62
40	2272.00	40	0.70
45	2556.00	45	0.79
50	2840.00	50	0.88
60	3408.00	60	1.06
70	3976.00	70	1.23
80	4544.00	80	1.41
90	5112.00	90	1.58
100	5680.00	100	1.76

PINTS TO LITRES

LITRES TO PINTS

multiply by 0.5680

multiply by 1.7600

pints	litres	litres	pints
0.25	0.14	0.25	0.44
0.5	0.28	0.5	0.88
0.75	0.43	0.75	1.32
1	0.57	1	1.76
2	1.14	2	3.52
3	1.70	3	5.28
4	2.27	4	7.04
5	2.84	5	8.80
6	3.41	6	10.56
7	3.98	7	12.32
8	4.54	8	14.08
9	5.11	9	15.84
10	5.68	10	17.60
11	6.25	11	19.36
12	6.82	12	21.12

pints	litres	litres	pints
13	7.38	13	22.88
14	7.95	14	24.64
15	8.52	15	26.40
16	9.09	16	28.16
17	9.66	17	29.92
18	10.22	18	31.68
19	10.79	19	33.44
20	11.36	20	35.20
25	14.20	25	44.00
30	17.04	30	52.80
35	19.88	35	61.60
40	22.72	40	70.40
45	25.56	45	79.20
50	28.40	50	88.00
60	34.08	60	105.60
70	39.76	70	123.20
80	45.44	80	140.80
90	51.12	90	158.40
100	56.80	100	176.00

QUARTS TO LITRES

LITRES TO QUARTS

multiply by 1.1365

multiply by 0.8798

quarts	litres	litres	quarts
0.25	0.28	0.25	0.22
0.5	0.57	0.5	0.44
0.75	0.85	0.75	0.66
1	1.14	1	0.88
2	2.27	2	1.76
3	3.41	3	2.64
4	4.55	4	3.52
5	5.68	5	4.40
6	6.82	6	5.28
7	7.96	7	6.16
8	9.09	8	7.04
9	10.23	9	7.92
10	11.37	10	8.80
11	12.50	11	9.68
12	13.64	12	10.56

quarts	litres	litres	quarts
13	14.77	13	11.44
14	15.91	14	12.32
15	17.05	15	13.20
16	18.18	16	14.08
17	19.32	17	14.96
18	20.46	18	15.84
19	21.59	19	16.72
20	22.73	20	17.60
25	28.41	25	22.00
30	34.10	30	26.39
35	39.78	35	30.79
40	45.46	40	35.19
45	51.14	45	39.59
50	56.83	50	43.99
60	68.19	60	52.79
70	79.56	70	61.59
80	90.92	80	70.38
90	102.29	90	79.18
100	113.65	100	87.98

GALLONS TO LITRES

LITRES TO GALLONS

multiply by 4.5400

multiply by 0.2200

gallons	litres	litres	gallons
0.25	1.14	0.25	0.06
0.5	2.27	0.5	0.11
0.75	3.41	0.75	0.17
1	4.54	1	0.22
2	9.08	2	0.44
3	13.62	3	0.66
4	18.16	4	0.88
5	22.70	5	1.10
6	27.24	6	1.32
7	31.78	7	1.54
8	36.32	8	1.76
9	40.86	9	1.98
10	45.40	10	2.20
11	49.94	11	2.42
12	54.48	12	2.64

gallons	litres	litres	gallons
13	59.02	13	2.86
14	63.56	14	3.08
15	68.10	15	3.30
16	72.64	16	3.52
17	77.18	17	3.74
18	81.72	18	3.96
19	86.26	19	4.18
20	90.80	20	4.40
25	113.50	25	5.50
30	136.20	30	6.60
35	158.90	35	7.70
40	181.60	40	8.80
45	204.30	45	9.90
50	227.00	50	11.00
60	272.40	60	13.20
70	317.80	70	15.40
80	363.20	80	17.60
90	408.60	90	19.80
100	454.00	100	22.00

WEIGHT
CONVERSION
TABLES

GRAINS TO GRAMS

GRAMS TO GRAINS

multiply by 0.0648

multiply by 15.4300

grains	grams	grams	grains
0.25	0.02	0.25	3.86
0.5	0.03	0.5	7.72
0.75	0.05	0.75	11.57
1	0.06	1	15.43
2	0.13	2	30.86
3	0.19	3	46.29
4	0.26	4	61.72
5	0.32	5	77.15
6	0.39	6	92.58
7	0.45	7	108.01
8	0.52	8	123.44
9	0.58	9	138.87
10	0.65	10	154.30
11	0.71	11	169.73
12	0.78	12	185.16

grains	grams	grams	grains
13	0.84	13	200.59
14	0.91	14	216.02
15	0.97	15	231.45
16	1.04	16	246.88
17	1.10	17	262.31
18	1.17	18	277.74
19	1.23	19	293.17
20	1.30	20	308.60
25	1.62	25	385.75
30	1.94	30	462.90
35	2.27	35	540.05
40	2.59	40	617.20
45	2.92	45	694.35
50	3.24	50	771.50
60	3.89	60	925.80
70	4.54	70	1080.10
80	5.18	80	1234.40
90	5.83	90	1388.70
100	6.48	100	1543.00

OUNCES TO GRAMS		GRAMS TO OUNCES	
multiply by 28.3500		*multiply by 0.0353*	
ounces	grams	grams	ounces
0.25	7.09	0.25	0.01
0.5	14.18	0.5	0.02
0.75	21.26	0.75	0.03
1	28.35	1	0.04
2	56.70	2	0.07
3	85.05	3	0.11
4	113.40	4	0.14
5	141.75	5	0.18
6	170.10	6	0.21
7	198.45	7	0.25
8	226.80	8	0.28
9	255.15	9	0.32
10	283.50	10	0.35
11	311.85	11	0.39
12	340.20	12	0.42

ounces	grams	grams	ounces
13	368.55	13	0.46
14	396.90	14	0.49
15	425.25	15	0.53
16	453.60	16	0.56
17	481.95	17	0.60
18	510.30	18	0.64
19	538.65	19	0.67
20	567.00	20	0.71
25	708.75	25	0.88
30	850.50	30	1.06
35	992.25	35	1.24
40	1134.00	40	1.41
45	1275.75	45	1.59
50	1417.50	50	1.77
60	1701.00	60	2.12
70	1984.50	70	2.47
80	2268.00	80	2.82
90	2551.50	90	3.18
100	2835.00	100	3.53

POUNDS TO KILOGRAMMES

multiply by 0.4536

KILOGRAMMES TO POUNDS

multiply by 2.2050

lbs	kilos	kilos	lbs
0.25	0.11	0.25	0.55
0.5	0.23	0.5	1.10
0.75	0.34	0.75	1.65
1	0.45	1	2.21
2	0.91	2	4.41
3	1.36	3	6.62
4	1.81	4	8.82
5	2.27	5	11.03
6	2.72	6	13.23
7	3.18	7	15.44
8	3.63	8	17.64
9	4.08	9	19.85
10	4.54	10	22.05
11	4.99	11	24.26
12	5.44	12	26.46

lbs	kilos	kilos	lbs
13	5.90	13	28.67
14	6.35	14	30.87
15	6.80	15	33.08
16	7.26	16	35.28
17	7.71	17	37.49
18	8.16	18	39.69
19	8.62	19	41.90
20	9.07	20	44.10
25	11.34	25	55.13
30	13.61	30	66.15
35	15.88	35	77.18
40	18.14	40	88.20
45	20.41	45	99.23
50	22.68	50	110.25
60	27.22	60	132.30
70	31.75	70	154.35
80	36.29	80	176.40
90	40.82	90	198.45
100	45.36	100	220.5

WEIGHT IN STONES & POUNDS TO KILOGRAMMES

WEIGHT IN KILOGRAMMES TO STONES & POUNDS

st & lbs	kilos	kilos	st & lbs
6 6	40.82	40	6 4
6 8	41.73	41	6 6
6 10	42.64	42	6 9
6 12	43.55	43	6 11
7 0	44.45	44	6 13
7 2	45.36	45	7 1
7 4	46.27	46	7 3
7 6	47.17	47	7 6
7 8	48.08	48	7 8
7 10	48.99	49	7 10
7 12	49.90	50	7 12
8 0	50.80	51	8 0
8 2	51.71	52	8 3
8 4	52.62	53	8 5
8 6	53.52	54	8 7

st & lbs	kilos	kilos	st & lbs
8 8	54.43	55	8 9
8 10	55.34	56	8 11
8 12	56.25	57	8 13
9 0	57.15	58	9 2
9 2	58.06	59	9 4
9 4	58.97	60	9 6
9 6	59.88	61	9 9
9 8	60.78	62	9 11
9 10	61.69	63	9 13
9 12	62.60	64	10 1
10 0	63.50	65	10 3
10 2	64.41	66	10 6
10 4	65.32	67	10 8
10 6	66.23	68	10 10
10 8	67.13	69	10 12
10 10	68.04	70	11 0
10 12	68.95	71	11 3
11 0	69.85	72	11 5
11 2	70.76	73	11 7
11 4	71.67	74	11 9

st & lbs	kilos	kilos	st & lbs
11 6	72.58	75	11 11
11 8	73.48	76	11 13
11 10	74.39	77	12 2
11 12	75.30	78	12 4
12 0	76.20	79	12 6
12 2	77.11	80	12 8
12 4	78.02	81	12 11
12 6	78.93	82	12 13
12 8	79.83	83	13 1
12 10	80.74	84	13 3
12 12	81.65	85	13 5
13 0	82.56	86	13 8
13 2	83.46	87	13 10
13 4	84.37	88	13 12
13 6	85.28	89	14 0
13 8	86.18	90	14 2
13 10	87.09	91	14 5
13 12	88.00	92	14 7
14 0	88.91	93	14 9
14 2	89.81	94	14 11

st & lbs	kilos	kilos	st & lbs
14 4	90.72	95	14 13
14 6	91.63	96	15 2
14 8	92.53	97	15 4
14 10	93.44	98	15 6
14 12	94.35	99	15 8
15 0	95.26	100	15 11
15 2	96.16	101	15 13
15 4	97.07	102	16 1
15 6	97.98	103	16 3
15 8	98.88	104	16 5
15 10	99.79	105	16 8
15 12	100.70	106	16 10
16 0	101.61	107	16 12
16 2	102.51	108	17 0
16 4	103.42	109	17 2
16 6	104.33	110	17 5
16 8	105.24	111	17 7
16 10	106.14	112	17 9
16 12	107.05	113	17 11
17 0	107.96	114	17 13

THE ESSENTIAL SERIES

Essential Dealing with Debt
by Ruth Parsons   ISBN 1-873432-49-6
Many people have to face up to being in debt at some time. This book helps you face the realities, negotiate and deal with your creditors and offers you an orderly escape route.

Essential Help Handbook – where to turn in a crisis
by Anthea Nichols   ISBN 1-873432-46-1
This book lists the comprehensive network of support groups that offer both immediate help and long term counselling.

Essential House Husbands' Handbook
by Michael Derbyshire   ISBN 1-873432-40-2
Many men now look after the home and children. This book organises housework, shopping, finances, childcare, cooking, laundry and simple first aid.

Essential Lone Parent Survival Guide
by Sue Slipman   ISBN 1-873432-34-8
All you need to know to survive as a lone parent. It addresses housing, law, taxation, maintenance, childcare, employment and where to find help.

Essential Safety Awareness for Women
by Julie Benjamin   ISBN 1-873432-37-2
This guide makes women aware of potential danger and how to diffuse it. It covers safety at home, in the car, at work, on public transport or just out and about and includes self-defence.

Available from bookshops or direct from
Boatswain Press Ltd
12 North Street, Emsworth, Hampshire PO10 7DQ
Please send £1.95 plus 36p postage per title